A Guide and Workbook

The Unplanned Career
How to Turn Curiosity into Opportunity

By Kathleen Mitchell

CHRONICLE BOOKS
SAN FRANCISCO

Design by Protopod Design
Illustrations by Jon Flaming
Manufactured in China

Library of Congress Cataloging-in-Publication Data

Mitchell, Kathleen (Kathleen E.)
  The unplanned career : turning curiosity into opportunity : a guide
and workbook / by Kathleen Mitchell.
     p. cm.
  ISBN 0-8118-3596-0
  1. Career development. 2. Diaries--Authorship. I. Title.
  HF5381M57 2003
  650.1--dc21
                                        2003006328

Distributed in Canada by
Raincoast Books
9050 Shaughnessy Street
Vancouver, B.C. V6P 6E5

10 9 8 7 6 5 4 3 2 1

Chronicle Books LLC
85 Second Street
San Francisco, CA 94105
www.chroniclebooks.com

Table of Contents

A New Look at Careers

If you've picked up this book, it's probably because you're looking for help thinking about your career. Maybe you've been in your career for a while and you're feeling dissatisfied or stuck, yet unsure about whether you can make a change because you don't know what to do next. You could be wondering about ways to make your work more challenging and fulfilling, but you don't know how to go about it. Perhaps you've decided to leave your current job and are facing an overwhelming search process. Or you're just starting out, with several career possibilities in front of you, and are uncertain how to choose among them.

Whatever your particular situation, your feelings of dissatisfaction may stem from the advice you've been given about career planning. Most people are brought up to think that they can and should plan their careers the way an architect designs a building. No one would think of constructing a house without having a plan in place. Similarly, the best approach to a career is to choose it and plan it in advance, and then carry out the plan step-by-step, right?

Not exactly. You are better off ignoring the traditional notion of career planning. Just as maps are made after the terrain has been traveled and photographs are developed after they have been taken, careers happen when you try something first and make sense of it later. In other words, you don't need to know what career you want or what you're good at before you set out.

The idea for this journal grew out of my twenty-year experience as a career counselor and consultant, working with hundreds of people who have made a career change or who have taken steps to begin their first career in a world that often expects maps before discovery. I have grown to understand from my clients' journeys that careers are seldom planned but are often developed by being aware of and acting on the landmarks that appear along the way.

Because life is often hectic, you may rarely have time to reflect on your career concerns. You may be too busy trying to find work or do the work you already have. Or you may feel bombarded with advice, whether helpful or inconsistent. This journal will provide a respite where you can contemplate what matters to you.

The journal represents a cyclical process. You can begin with the chapter that is the most useful to you. Start with Chapter 1, "The Unplanned Career," if you are preparing to enter your first career or are considering changing careers, for instance, or Chapter 3, "Directing Your Job Search," if you are seeking employment. You can skip parts of the journal and return to them later as they become relevant to your journey.

Throughout the journal, I pose questions for you to reflect on and write about. You won't just be talked to and given information; you will be asked to write down your thoughts, your struggles, and your progress. You'll also see that I've included anecdotes to clarify a point or encourage you. These stories are from my clients and students or people I've interviewed who graciously consented to let me share their experiences (and whose names have been changed to protect their privacy).

You may feel overwhelmed about the journey that lies ahead. But if you proceed a bit at a time, you can keep moving forward. A line from *Aesop's Fables* says, "Little by little does the trick." A lot can be accomplished in small blocks of time. Feel free to write as much or as little as you like in your journal each time you open it. Writing for five minutes a day or twenty minutes each week—perhaps before you begin your day or at lunchtime—will keep you motivated.

This journal will be your unique creation. It will remain yours to consult in the future for encouragement, allowing you to be inspired by your own words. Ultimately, this journal will enable you to be the creator of your own career.

 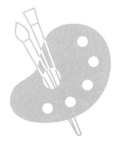 

"Any damned fool can write a plan. It's the execution that gets you all screwed up."

—James F. Hollingsworth

Chapter 1

The Unplanned Career

You are not a "damned fool" if you have set out to create a career from a plan. But you may have been made to feel foolish by others who put pressure on you to keep to a plan you know isn't right for you.

This chapter will help release you from those pressures or help you avoid them. The myths you believe and the thoughts you hold can encourage you to explore your curiosity or block you by fear. You'll be given an opportunity to review your career myths and thoughts, and even your career values, and revise them if they have been holding you back.

The poet Carl Sandburg said, "Nearly all the best things that came to me in life have been unexpected, unplanned by me." An unplanned career is full of opportunity. Your curiosity will lead you to your unplanned career. This chapter will guide you to take action on your curiosity and to note your interests along the way. You'll be encouraged to look into your ideas without the pressure to decide or eliminate anything.

Easing the Pressure to Decide

"Decisions, particularly important ones, have always made me sleepy, perhaps because I know that I will have to make them by instinct, and thinking things out is only what other people tell me I should do."

—LILLIAN HELLMAN

Many people have inherited distorted ideas about career planning, but the most persistent—and the one you should dispense with first—is that you need a plan before you can make a career. Planning a career has become the preferred pastime for people discouraged from beginning or changing a career. The very idea of planning can actually be a distraction from creating career options, and waiting for a career plan to form allows excess time for negative predictions about the future. The more people plan, the more they become convinced that they should settle only for the perfect career. Therefore, if you don't want a career, spend time planning it.

On the other hand, if you do want a career, you're likely to trip over it while you are doing something other than planning. History is filled with examples of careers that sprang from action. People have launched careers while they were busy making scientific discoveries, coming up with new inventions, and creating music and literature.

If you are like most people, your first introduction to career planning was when you were asked, "What do you want to be when you grow up?" Like most kids, to please adults, you answered with a response like doctor, lawyer, astronaut, or whatever career was popular at the moment. Not surprisingly, you were left with a limited view of what is available to you and with the notion that careers just magically happen.

As you grew up, you may have faced a parade of similar questions: "What's your major?" "What will you do with your major?" "If you quit your job, what will you do next?" On the surface, there's nothing wrong with such questions, but you probably noticed that when you responded with a job title, most questioners were satisfied. You discovered that job titles could offer sanctuary—but not for long. Soon new pressures arose for you to begin preparing for the career, and that's when the problems really began. Perhaps you felt pushed to move forward into a field you may not have wanted, or you didn't want to risk looking indecisive by changing your mind. Either way, you were trapped.

Look at how Allen dealt with a similar dilemma. Ever since he was a child, his father had encouraged him to become an engineer. If Allen brought up other career ideas, his father would dismiss them as impractical.

A few semesters into his studies, Allen told his father that he was dropping out of the engineering program to work in an unrelated field. He became interested in this new field when he took an elective in sculpture and found it more creative than engineering. A classmate mentioned to Allen that a theater group was looking for help designing sets and props. Allen applied, got the job, and worked as an apprentice. Having learned a lot from his mentors, he went on to take numerous jobs where he perfected his skills. He eventually opened his own business, which now employs a staff of artists to design and create sets, props, and displays for large and small events around the country.

Allen risked a great deal, but he gained much more. His father was not wrong to want his son to become an engineer, and Allen did not make a mistake by going along with it. Job titles are not always bad. The error was putting pressure on Allen to accept a job title before he had a chance to explore other options.

If you feel you decided your career too soon or made a mistake in the direction you chose, first let up the pressure on yourself. There is no right or wrong decision. What counts is how you revise the decision and adjust it to fit better.

Rewriting Career Myths

"If the Sun and the Moon should doubt,
 They'd immediately go out."
—WILLIAM BLAKE

Behind most efforts to plan a career is the desire to change something you've been doing. Numerous attempts to do that prove your resolve, not your failure. You deserve time and encouragement to explore your interests. If you start looking, then stop before you are satisfied, a career myth may need to be updated.

The good news about myths is that they can be rewritten. Consider the following myths and their revisions:

Myth: I need a perfect career plan before I can begin exploring.

Revision: I don't need every detail mapped out before I start to look into my career interests. I want to make room for new opportunities that I might discover. If my plan is too inflexible, I might miss those opportunities.

Myth: Once I decide on a career, I've got to stick with it.

Revision: I'm not willing to stay with something that makes me miserable. If after a while I decide I want to change to another field, I am confident that I have the knowledge and ability to make that happen.

Have career myths been directing your thoughts? Write down one or two myths that have been holding you back, then compose revisions.

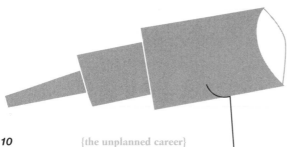

Challenging the Thoughts
That Limit You

"No passion so effectually robs the mind of all its powers
of acting and reasoning as fear."

—EDMUND BURKE

When you consider career options, thoughts of a confining past or an uncertain future may shackle your ideas before they can take form. Perhaps you worry about confronting unemployment or financial ruin before you have a chance to begin a career or make a career change. Or perhaps you spend time revisiting the past, reviewing all the things you didn't do that now prevent you from doing what you really want. The natural result is an attitude of "why bother?"

Accepting limiting thoughts means they have won, and your wonder and curiosity have lost. You may dismiss career options because you don't believe in yourself. You may seek out people who confirm your fears, the doomsday sages, and ignore those who challenge your limiting thoughts. You convince yourself that you are right not to try.

The truth is, your fears are not entirely false. No one wants to fail or waste time or money while pursuing unfeasible ideas. When jobs seem hard to come by and friends have been laid off, you feel foolish considering anything other than what you have. "Be happy that you have a job," you tell yourself. But that gnawing feeling continues. You know you want something more. Trapped in a slump, you wonder, "How do I justify giving up what I have for something that might fail?"

The answer is, you don't have to justify anything, because you have given up nothing. The first step is just to look up and around. The thoughts that restrain you can't predict a thing.

Embedded in most constraining thoughts is the belief that something you want *won't* happen because something else *will* happen. For example, you think, "I won't have a chance in that field because they'll think I'm too old," or "I can't enroll in that program because it will cost too much."

What would happen if you consider that you might be misinformed about what won't and will happen? What would change, for example, if you held this thought: "I might be able to enroll in that program if I look into how I could manage it financially." Or, "Just how is age viewed in that field, and whom could I ask?"

You might discover that the program is prohibitively expensive and that the field often has an age ceiling. On the other hand, you might learn that the program offers scholarships and that your previous experience is what the field needs. Rephrasing your assumptions and restraining thoughts as questions helps you go out and look around.

Begin practicing this technique of rephrasing. Listen to your thoughts and try to identify the assumptions they contain. Thoughts that come packaged in negative terms—what "can't" or "won't" happen—deserve particular attention. Pick one or two limiting thoughts you might have, such as "I don't have enough education to get into that career," and make them into questions. For example, your revision might read, "How much education does a person need in this career? Where can I go to find out?"

Questioning Your Career Values

—RALPH WALDO EMERSON

Career values are shaped by experiences. From your life and work experiences, you form values about the qualities you want in bosses and coworkers, about the work you want to do and not do, about the pay you desire, and about where and how you want to work. As an example, you might value flexible hours rather than a more structured schedule. Therefore, when considering career options, you become drawn to work settings that are adaptable rather than limited.

Career values are sometimes the starting place when considering work options. They can guide you into work that is satisfying, and they can also remind you of what you don't want in your work. But career values can play another role—one that keeps you from doing more satisfying work.

Tom is in his mid-thirties but can describe his first public speaking experience as if it happened yesterday. The student body of his school was assembled for the annual homecoming play. Tom had a lead role. When he came onstage, he blanked on his opening sentence. Although a friend came to his rescue and reminded him of his lines, the damage was done. He finished his performance and vowed never to put himself in such a situation again. Tom's career choice was impacted by that experience: He chose accounting because it matched the value he placed on working primarily by himself.

Although Tom's career values made sense for many years, he gradually felt isolated. He fantasized about pursuing a career with more people contact, but his fear of public speaking prevented him from exploring other options. Then, through volunteer work with a research institute, he discovered that he was skilled at interviewing people and consolidating their comments into reports. When offered a job with the institute, he nearly turned it down because it required him to present his findings to groups. Tom then knew he had to confront his earlier experience and take a speech class. He also had to update his career values.

Like Tom, you may need to look at the fears behind some of your career values. Although your values are important to you and may assist you in positive ways, they may need fine-tuning, especially if you have begun to feel stuck in your work and think you have no other options.

Can you think of career values that might be hiding fears? Are there activities you have put aside because of fears, or are there situations you have avoided because of fear of failure? Write about those fears and what values might be masking them.

It has been said that a value is truly a value only when it has been tested. Many people can name the values that are important to them because they have learned through their experiences what matters and what does not. But the career values people don't want often go untested and, as a result, hold power over career selection.

Perhaps you don't think you will be successful at something, and to protect yourself from failing, you reject a career value. By avoiding openings for high-paying jobs, for instance, you don't apply for work that may require more skills than you think you have. In other words, you don't feel that what you have to offer or could learn to offer is worth a good salary. A negative experience or harsh words from someone may have convinced you to put a ceiling on your skill development and earning potential.

Or perhaps you have avoided pursuing a career that, in your mind, is associated with a highly competitive environment. You may have been in a job or other situation in the past where competition prevented you from learning, from thriving in your employment, or from working effectively with others.

If you have been avoiding careers because of your fear of competition or another untested career value, you will find it useful to step out from behind this value long enough to delve into its origins and examine if the value no longer matches the person you are becoming. Are there any career values that you have been convinced that you *don't* want? List a few below, and discuss whether there is room for one or two of these values in your life now.

The Comparison Game

—THORNTON WILDER

It may happen without warning. You find yourself wishing that you'd followed a
different path, been a better student, chosen a different major, or moved into a
different career. The paths others took can seem much more promising than the
one you pursued. Comparing yourself to others is what you do when you mourn
the past and doubt the future. It is a holding tank where you go to decide whether
you want to give up or move forward. However, instead of being a waste of energy,
comparisons can be useful if viewed as what could be instead of what is not.

When you start concentrating on someone who does work you view as more creative
than yours, do not find fault with yourself by comparison. Instead, ask yourself
how you might bring more creativity to your career. If you fixate on someone who
is making more money than you, do not belittle yourself. Instead, think of skills
you want to acquire that will be interesting to you and valuable to an employer,
and thereby increase your earnings. Turn the comparisons into statements about
how you can achieve what you feel is missing. In this way, what you *can* do to
enhance your career becomes more important than what you *didn't* do.

**When you make comparisons, what topics keep surfacing: money, educa-
tion, responsibility, accomplishments, success? Write down one or two
comparisons that you find yourself making, then rewrite them to reflect
changes you want to make.**

The Qualifications Trap

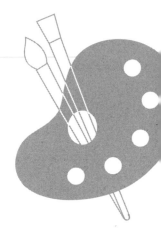

"There are two classes of people who tell what is going to happen in the future: Those who don't know, and those who don't know they don't know."

—JOHN KENNETH GALBRAITH

Whether you are seeking your first job or you are looking for a new job, you might dismiss interesting work opportunities because they are not a perfect match to your qualifications. You become convinced that employers will see only what you lack.

Fixated on applying only for jobs you think you're qualified for, you forget that most job descriptions are wish lists of qualifications. Employers include every- thing in the hope of attracting the ideal person. When that person does not emerge, the employer takes the next most qualified applicant or the one with the most promise to learn what the job takes. Unfortunately, you have already removed yourself from the running because you decided you don't have the exact qualifications. You may have been right about the qualifications, but you were wrong about the missed opportunity.

Consider how many times you've avoided applying for certain jobs because you thought your skills didn't match the qualifications. The problem may not be your lack of skills, but that you don't know the words to describe the skills you have. For example, someone who can effectively organize events might unknowingly downplay the ability as "just something I like doing," instead of recognizing it as event planning. Or someone who excels at troubleshooting might shrug it off by saying, "I just like to fix things."

Many people cut corners when talking about their skills. They often jump to the end result instead of noting the important steps they took to get there. Event planning, for example, takes many steps. Breaking down the process into the skills that led to the event can reveal how these skills are suitable for other kinds of work.

Do you feel that you lack the qualifications for work you'd really like to do? To explore this question, look for the description of a position that interests you. Think about how your experiences qualify you for the job, and sketch out those skills.

{the unplanned career}

Letting Curiosity Be Your Guide

"It is more important to pave the way for the child to want to know
than to put him on a diet of facts he is not ready to assimilate."

—RACHEL CARSON

People are not born certain—they are born curious. Children use all their senses to explore the world around them before they can come to understand it. But adults are expected to bypass their curiosity and have their lives in order. To be curious as an adult is risky. It is associated with wasting time or with uncertainty. However, when you are grappling with which career to choose, curiosity is essential. You need to allow time to look around and give yourself permission to learn about things you want to know, not necessarily because the knowledge will lead directly to a career or a specific job. On the other hand, what you learn by following your curiosity may be called upon in unexpected ways.

Consider Sharon, who in the process of creating her career drew on her memories of her childhood. She would walk along the sand with her grandmother, who explained the various life forms found in the ocean. As an adult, Sharon recalled her early fascination with the sounds and smells of the ocean and how soothed she felt by her grandmother's descriptions. She decided to reengage her curiosity about biology and oceanography, which eventually transformed into a career interest when she decided to enter the field of marine biology.

When you come to trust your curiosity, as Sharon did, you can explore career interests with an open mind. Perhaps, however, you have forfeited your curiosity for certainty, thinking that you could control your life if you would just make practical and realistic career decisions. Also, when money is involved and mortgages or rent must be paid, experimentation is regarded as too time-consuming or a distraction from getting on with serious career interests. If you follow this thinking, you'll run the risk of missing enriching opportunities.

Think about your career curiosities and write them as single words or short sentences. For example, words such as *writer, sales, movies, own business, boats,* or *machines* might come to mind. You also might express your curiosity by writing "I have always admired writers," or "I think I would be really good at sales," or "I've always wondered about owning my own

business." Don't worry about whether or not you'll actually pursue these ideas. Include as many curiosities as you would like.

{the unplanned career}

When a curiosity surfaces, it is prone to drop back underground if you don't do anything about it. To keep your curiosity alive and your willingness to look into your career ideas fresh, you need to come up with safe and enjoyable ways to investigate your curiosity.

For example, if you admire writers, is there a lecture series you could attend to hear about the experiences of professional authors? If you're curious about movies, do you have a knowledgeable friend who would see films with you and discuss them afterward? If you have a growing interest in technology or art, is there a place you could visit or someone you could talk to about your curiosity?

When you are ready, visit the place or talk with the person and write about what it was like for you to explore your curiosity free of expectations or judgments.

"Action and becoming are one."

—Meister Eckehart

Chapter 2

Taking Action

Taking action means looking into something. It is not the same as deciding on a career. The two steps are very different. If you've become blocked from exploring your curiosity, you just may have confused taking action with making a decision.

This chapter will help you look into your areas of curiosity without pressuring you to decide on a career. When you take action on your curiosity, you'll create career opportunities instead of make decisions. You'll be encouraged to follow up on these opportunities by talking with people and gathering information. Throughout the process, you'll be invited to record your findings and your reflections in your journal.

Planned Happenstance®

Your life is filled with unexpected events: an e-mail from a friend tells you about a job opportunity; a former boss calls to say she has started her own company and asks if you would like to join her; a program that you saw publicized causes you to wonder if you could enroll; a magazine responds to the query letter you sent months ago and had written off because so much time had passed. To act on such unanticipated opportunities, you need to be ready and willing.

The expression "planned happenstance" may be an oxymoron, but the two words represent what many people know to be true—behind the beginning of many careers lie some planning and some chance. The key is to be well prepared and open to the opportunities presented by chance events. Planned Happenstance is a career-counseling process whose premise is that you can create and transform the unexpected into career opportunities.

Although Nelson always liked science, other interests pulled him away, and he became a professional dancer after high school. Following many years of successful performances, he took a job in ground operations for a national delivery service that was developing its new tracking system. He became fascinated with the system's ability to locate packages anywhere in the United States. During his free time, Nelson raised parrots, which required him to do scientific research.

When Nelson's company transferred him to San Francisco, he became interested in returning to college to study biotechnology. He enrolled, graduated, and decided to find part-time work to see how he liked the field before he quit his job. As it turned out, he was hired by a biotechnology firm because of his parrots. Nelson had mentioned in the interview that caring for his parrots involved injecting them with medicines. Because injections were part of the biotechnology job, the company picked Nelson over the other candidates.

After two years, Nelson decided to look for full-time employment and applied at a large research hospital. During the interview, he described his work with a national tracking system. A person on the interviewing committee passed Nelson's resumé to a department involved with DNA research. The department created a position for him because they needed both his biotechnology training and his ability to set up a tracking system for DNA samples. Nelson attributed his success in entering biotechnology to luck. But as you review his actions, you'll see that Nelson created his own luck. Like Nelson, you can be prepared for unexpected opportunities that you can transform into "career luck."

Let others in on what you know. In everything he did, Nelson did his best to learn new skills. In his job interviews, he talked about his skills and experiences, and he made sure interviewers saw how they connected to the requirements of the position for which he was applying.

Take advantage of new learning opportunities. Sometimes you can become so caught up in your current work that you neglect to notice new opportunities to learn. Just as Nelson couldn't predict that his knowledge of a tracking system or his research into parrots would help him begin his new career in science, you won't always know where your knowledge will take you. But that shouldn't stop you from learning. Your knowledge will make you ready to act on unanticipated career opportunities.

Be willing to act on unexpected opportunities. Ralph Waldo Emerson said, "Good luck is another name for tenacity of purpose." Putting the *happen* in *happenstance* means taking steps that aren't always part of a path. Observe and notice the unexpected things that happen in your life and be willing to act on them even if you can't see how they will turn out.

In Chapter 1, "The Unplanned Career," when you looked into your curiosity, did you come across some unexpected leads? Did someone call you with information about an upcoming event related to your curiosity? Did you find a program that you want to know more about? Write down the steps you could take to follow up on unexpected events that occurred while you were exploring your curiosity.

Interviewing for Information

"Good conversation unrolls itself like the spring or like the dawn."
—W. B. YEATS

A good way to follow up on your curiosity is by talking with people about it. The informational interview is a dialogue you have with someone who is familiar with the object of your curiosity. This process is different from a job interview because you are only gathering information; you aren't applying for a job.

Knowing this distinction can help take pressure off you because you don't have to prove anything or convince someone of your qualifications. Your role is to prepare questions to ask and record useful information.

Consider interviewing relatives, friends, acquaintances, friends of friends, or anyone else you think might be a helpful resource. Explain to the person that you have prepared questions and that you'd like to meet for a specified time to discuss them.

Before the informational interview, select the questions that matter to you. For example, if you're interviewing a writer, and in the past you've had a difficult time adhering to a writing schedule, ask how the writer developed such a schedule and stuck to it. Or, if you're interviewing a small-business owner, and you've wondered how an idea can transform into a business, ask the person to explain the process.

In informational interviews, well-meaning people sometimes start offering advice rather than sharing information. If that happens, politely explain that you are just gathering information and have not yet decided on a career field. This is a reminder as much to yourself as to the person you're interviewing. When the interview shifts like this, you can become discouraged, usually because of the crossover from dialogue to decision making. Be alert to it, and steer the conversation back to useful topics.

Which areas of curiosity would you like to explore through informational interviews? Can you think of two to four people you could interview who are familiar with your area of curiosity? Set up times for informational interviews with them. (Note that by selecting certain areas, you're not ruling out others you might discover later. Nor are you deciding your career.)

{the unplanned career}

Use the space below to prepare questions for your informational interview. After the interview, record not only the information shared with you, but also your reflections on what you discussed.

Gaining Skills in Different Settings

"Skill to do comes of doing."
—RALPH WALDO EMERSON

You probably don't remember hearing the word *skill*, or being asked about your skills, when you were a child. You just did things and you learned. For example, you did not go to a lecture on the art of kicking a ball before you kicked one. Nor were you asked to assess your qualifications to kick.

When you entered the world of competitive sports, however, you may have heard statements like "Show us what you can do" or "You have to be better than the competition to get anywhere." As you looked around, you saw other eager kids, all wanting what you wanted, and all being judged on how well they did. For the first time, trying and learning by doing were not enough; you had to be the best at what you did to win.

Now that you are in the adult world of choosing or changing a career, you may be holding on to some of those earlier concerns about proving yourself, and you may be discouraged from seeking the work you want for fear that others are better qualified and have more skills.

One very useful way to gain skills is putting yourself in a situation where you can learn by doing. You do not need to develop skills perfectly the first time out. Instead, consider learning skills through a series of small steps.

Elizabeth had been an art student in college. After graduating, she worked in the field but grew tired of her job. To relieve the boredom, she would hang out at a local restaurant. One day, the owner asked if she would like to work there, and she accepted.

Elizabeth wondered why the owner sold baked goods prepared by outside vendors instead of baking his own. She volunteered to bake the pastries and was surprised to find that baking fascinated her. To learn more, she volunteered in another restaurant with an experienced pastry chef. Because of this volunteer experience, she was offered a full-time paid position as an assistant pastry chef at an upscale restaurant. While working there, she visited a newly opened restaurant and convinced the head chef that the pastry could be far better than it was. The chef offered her a position, which she accepted. Eventually, Elizabeth opened her own successful restaurant.

Elizabeth's experience provides a template for how you can develop skills in different settings by taking a series of steps linked by a willingness to try something new. Elizabeth suspended her need to be perfect and replaced it with curiosity. She was always on the lookout for new things to learn, and when she exhausted a learning opportunity, she moved on to a new one.

If you are unable to work full- or part-time to develop new skills, you might try volunteering or interning in an area related to your curiosity. The experience might include mentoring or training that provides additional guidance in developing skills. Be sure that volunteering or interning fits into your life. If you cram something else into an already busy schedule, you can become discouraged. Instead, consider modifying what you're doing to make room for what you'd like to learn.

If you want to learn about animals, volunteer at a zoo or an animal shelter. Check out opportunities in schools, if teaching interests you. Many nonprofit organizations need help with technology and can't afford additional staff, but are willing to train interns. Some companies offer time off to employees who volunteer for a nonprofit. If you are concerned about a social or community issue, investigate who is sponsoring events and offer to help. Community organizations rely on volunteers, and they need people who share their passion and concerns.

Check your local volunteer bureau for ideas or call organizations that interest you to find opportunities for volunteering or interning. Many companies welcome short-term interns willing to work just a few hours a week. Schools and job organizations can help you connect with an appropriate company offering an internship program. Even a few hours a month of volunteering or interning can assist you in meeting new people, developing new skills, and engaging in work that fulfills your curiosity. Keeping the internship short (say, three months) ensures that you can explore something else if you want and that the company doesn't take advantage of you. Some companies and organizations require prospective volunteers and interns to follow an application process similar to that for those seeking full-time employment. For help with resumés and interviews, you'll want to consult Chapter 3, "Directing Your Job Search" (page 63).

Where could you volunteer or intern to learn more about your area of curiosity and gain additional skills? Record the names of places you'd like to approach and sketch out ideas for the work you'd like to try.

Seeking Out Resources

"Each day grow older and learn something new."
—SOLON

Using resources such as reference books, directories, and Web sites, you can find names of professional organizations, union information, and internship and volunteer opportunities related to your areas of curiosity.

Public libraries contain directories that list businesses by products and services. Likewise, you'll find social-service directories containing nonprofit organizations by population served and services provided. Many of these resources are online and can be found through your favorite search engine. You'll also find a selection of useful Web sites at the back of this book (page 160). Many libraries subscribe to professional journals and publications that may be relevant to your field of interest.

Do not hesitate to utilize the services of reference librarians. Not only are they experts in information retrieval, but they can help you clarify your questions and find resources most appropriate to your search.

Both public and college libraries generally offer Internet access; however, many require that you have a library card or student identification. Membership may also entitle you to access library databases remotely through your own computer.

Many community college career centers allow nonstudents to use their services for limited visits; some may charge a small access fee. There you'll find computerized information including career descriptions, preparation required, salary ranges, volunteer opportunities, and employment trends for fields listed by geographic areas.

Much as you did when you prepared for the informational interview, you should approach all these resources with prepared questions. Your questions will guide you to useful resources and eliminate those that aren't.

As you utilize various resources, record your questions and findings. Keep track of the name of the resource, where you found it, and the information you unearthed. Record your reflections on the information you discovered.

Money Matters

Money is an important part of living. No one wants to struggle throughout life to pay the bills, but no one can predict how much money can be made in a career. Although salary projections are potentially helpful, they can cause you to limit your options. Many resources state salary ranges that may be discouraging to someone starting out in a career or changing to another. These ranges are not always accurate, nor do they account for unexpected income-generating opportunities that you may create in your work.

Consider Bill, a high school teacher who nearly passed up teaching as a career because of the low salary he thought he would make. Despite his misgivings about the salary, he tried student teaching and found that he loved the students and the work. His student teaching led to an offer of permanent teaching, which he accepted, fully expecting that the salary would cause him to leave after a few years.

While teaching creative writing to his students, Bill practiced his own writing. He began to write about his travels during the summer and submitted his articles to travel magazines. One magazine printed them and encouraged him to travel and write more at its expense. His summers away from teaching are now filled with travel and writing opportunities. Not only has Bill's income increased, but he also created an opportunity to develop his interest and skill in writing. Furthermore, he has traveled to places he would not have been able to afford on his teaching salary.

Bill's experience brings up another issue that you might be concerned about as you investigate your curiosity. You may not want to pursue only one field as a career. You may dread becoming bored with doing the same job over and over. If this is the case, consider investigating how you can express your interests in more than one form of work, while also increasing your income possibilities.

As you come across financial information about one or more of your areas of curiosity, record your findings and your reflections. Also write about ways in which your multiple interests could help you generate income.

{the unplanned career}

Building a Support Network

"Those who believe in our ability do more than stimulate us.
They create for us an atmosphere in which it becomes easier
to succeed."

—JOHN LANCASTER SPALDING

The people you want in your support network are your advocates. They believe in you and they want you to succeed. Also in your network are people who can help you by sharing information and resources.

Your support system can include members of your family, past and present coworkers or bosses, a career counselor, or perhaps an Internet chat room. Someone you met while exploring your curiosity could become part of your network.

Check in with the people in your support network throughout your exploration, especially if you become discouraged. Talking with an advocate can help get you back on track.

Record the names of people you'd like to include in your support system. When you have a conversation, keep track of it in your journal, noting the words of encouragement you receive so you can refer to them later when you need a boost.

"Experience is something you get looking for something else."

—Mary Pettibone Poole

{Chapter 3}
Directing Your Job Search

You've been taking action by exploring your areas of curiosity, doing informational interviews, gaining skills, consulting resources, and building a support network. You've reflected on your findings and now may feel ready to seek employment in a field related to your area of curiosity.

This chapter will help guide you through your job search, from generating job leads to constructing your resumé and interviewing with prospective employers. You'll be asked to adopt the outlook that every lead is worth investigating, even if you can't anticipate the results of your efforts. Having an open mind that views chance events as opportunities—and having the persistence to follow up on them—can be as useful as a well-written resumé or clever answers to interview questions. Your journal will provide you with encouragement to create a job search that places you in the right place at the right time.

Many companies today expect volunteers and interns to follow the same application process as people seeking paid employment. Therefore, the discussion about developing contacts and leads, constructing resumés, compiling references, and participating in interviews will be useful whether you are searching for a full-time job, part-time work, an internship, or volunteer work.

Your work is continually to find ways to explore your curiosity. View your first job or the new one you are seeking as an opportunity to learn, gain skills, and grow through the experience.

Networking with Informed Contacts

"If you would know the road ahead, ask someone who has traveled it."
—CHINESE PROVERB

By far the most useful way to discover job opportunities is by asking around. People are rich resources of information. Tell them you're seeking a position in your area of curiosity or looking to change from the work you've been doing. Do not feel you are burdening people by asking for their assistance—most people want to help if asked.

If you have been laid off or lost your job for other reasons, try not to let embarrassment keep you from asking where to look for new opportunities. Most people have experienced some form of loss or setback, and they realize the importance of support and encouragement.

Your informed contacts could be colleagues from work or former coworkers, people you met through interning or volunteering, and people with whom you had informational interviews. You may find informed contacts among your support network, such as family members and friends who may have a connection to your field of interest. Be broad and creative in your thinking. For instance, people you know through school or your alumni association or people you met through hobbies or religious activities are potential employers and can provide job leads.

In your search for employment, your tendency might be to use job titles. If you have a job title in mind and you know it's what you want, certainly use it when talking to your contacts. On the other hand, if you know what you want to do but don't know what to call it, avoid specific titles and instead mention the activities you are interested in doing.

For example, Sandra worked in finance for many years. She wanted her new work to have a direct impact on people. She described her curiosity this way: "I believe that with accurate guidance in managing money, people can learn to take control of their lives and build successful businesses. I am interested in helping people in third world countries set up small businesses. Do you know people or organizations involved in such work?" Sandra avoided using the job title "foreign investor," because she wanted to explore broader options than working solely with financial institutions. By not pigeonholing yourself with a job title, you'll create room for those unexpected suggestions that might lead you to exciting opportunities.

Ask your contacts for advice on the most appropriate method to follow up on their leads. Depending on the situation, it may be more effective to call, e-mail, or send a resumé. At some companies, sending a resumé may be standard. At more informal places, an e-mail may get a quick response. Sometimes a personal call is best, but in other cases people may be too busy to return calls directly and prefer e-mail.

Follow up on every lead, even if you don't think it will go anywhere. Be sure to explore surprises—those unexpected tips you received from your contacts and from other people you met while pursuing leads. You just might create "the right place at the right time."

Remember to send an e-mail or written note to your contacts thanking them for their help. In your correspondence, mention how you took advantage of their leads. Be alert for ways to return the contacts' favors.

List the names of your informed contacts. Next to each name, write down leads they might be able to provide, for example, "Rosa: may know about special education. John: worked for a financial advisor."

Once you've begun to get in touch with these contacts above, note the date and any leads and other useful information they gave you. Jot down information they shared, for example, "Rosa: director of training position opening up at the company where her sister works," or "John: cousin looking for an assistant to help with conferences." Include your follow-up to the information provided by your contacts—whether you called, e-mailed, sent a resumé, or set up an appointment—and the results.

Contact:

Date:

Leads:

Action Taken:

Contact:

Date:

Leads:

Action Taken:

Contact:

Date:

Leads:

Action Taken:

Contact:

Date:

Leads:

Action Taken:

Contact:

Date:

Leads:

Action Taken:

Contact:

Date:

Leads:

Action Taken:

Contact:

Date:

Leads:

Action Taken:

Contact:

Date:

Leads:

Action Taken:

Contact:

Date:

Leads:

Action Taken:

Contact:

Date:

Leads:

Action Taken:

Contact:

Date:

Leads:

Action Taken:

Researching Job Sources

"We are wiser than we know."

—RALPH WALDO EMERSON

Another valuable source for job opportunities is the Internet. Browse through some of the sites listed in the Resources section of this journal (page 158). By far the most comprehensive resource for printed and online information is *The Riley Guide*. There you'll find everything you need to know about job listings, networking, targeting and researching employers, resumés and cover letters, interviewing, and negotiating a salary, as well as links to hundreds of other useful resources. Browse through the listings, note those relevant to your search, read what *The Riley Guide* has to say about each one, and record those of particular interest to you.

Don't forget to investigate local newspapers and the journals, newsletters, and job listings of various trade associations for employment opportunities. As you investigate resources, record those that are most useful to you and the job leads they provide.

{the unplanned career}

Constructing Your Resumé

The main purpose of a resumé is to summarize your work history. The resumé you compose in this journal can serve another purpose as well. It can become your master resumé from which you can draw when building a resumé for a specific position. Always keep your master resumé current by updating it after each paid or unpaid job you've held or major project you've completed.

Start by thinking about your job objective, or compose a single statement that describes the work you'd like to do. Even if you don't include an objective in your resumé, writing one can help you gain clarity about the work you would like. It can be general or it can be very specific. Avoid wording your objective with statements such as "Seeking a fulfilling position" or "I want a position where I can grow and develop."

Tony, who worked as a technical writer for five years, wanted to volunteer in an animal shelter to determine if he'd like the field before he sought education and training as a veterinarian. Here's how he worded his objective: "A volunteer opportunity with [name of shelter] where I can apply my respect for animals and gain insight into the qualities that make a competent and caring veterinarian." Yvonne, a recent college graduate in visual arts, was seeking paid employment with a design firm. She wrote this objective on her resumé: "A position in graphic design with [name of company] where I will contribute my recent education and training in computer graphics and animation."

Review the models in the selected resources in this journal and consult your informed contacts to determine if inclusion of an objective in your resumé is standard for your field. Try writing an objective below.

An initial step in building your resumé is to list all the positions you've held and describe what you did while in them. As you assemble the list, include not only your paid positions but also your volunteer work and internships. Record details that would help a reader understand the range of your experience. For example, "managed a team of fifty sales representatives from thirty regions across the state" tells the reader much more about your responsibilities than "managed sales representatives." Rather than state that you *designed* a project, highlight each phase of the process in which you were involved, using active verbs like *conceptualized, implemented*, and *evaluated*. When you're describing your skills, it's best to avoid such phrases as "strong leadership skills" or "strong decision-maker." Instead, give examples of the projects you led and the decisions you made.

Use the following space to detail your work history. Add to this section when you want to update your master resumé.

{the unplanned career}

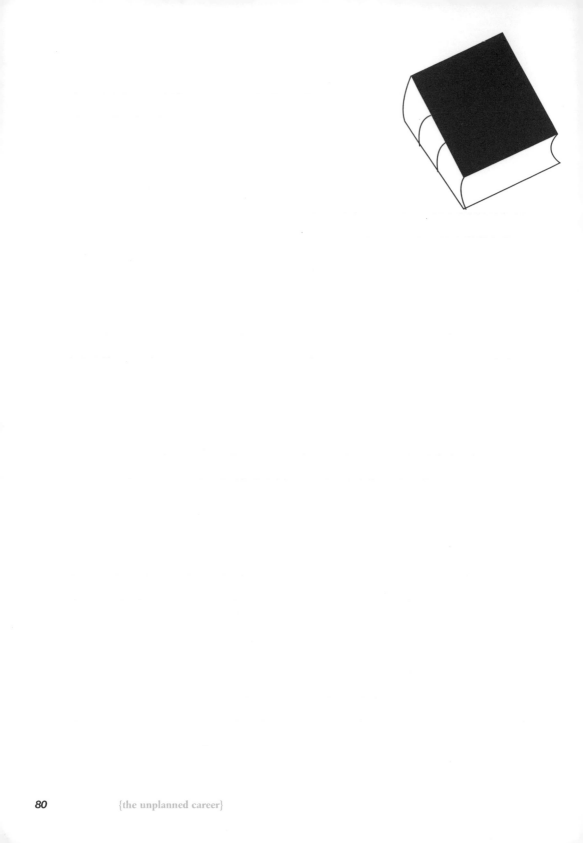

{the unplanned career}

Once you've finished writing about your work history, record your education. Include degrees completed, seminars taken, certificates achieved, or training in which you participated.

{the unplanned career}

Your next step is to determine the layout of your resumé. Does your education, work experience, or community involvement best demonstrate your qualifications for the position? Organize your resumé so your best qualifications appear first. Keep in mind the job description as you build your resumé. For example, if management experience is required and you have it, clearly state this at the start (as well as in your cover letter) so that the recipient will quickly notice that you have the necessary qualifications. On the other hand, for some positions, giving prominence to your education is important.

Sometimes it's useful to break your work history into two categories, such as "Related Work Experience," where you list work directly related to the position, and "Additional Work Experience," where you list extra skills acquired from other work you've done. Whether or not you use multiple categories, your resumé should be kept to one or, at the most, two pages. This means that the final resumé will need to emphasize your education and work history most relevant to the position for which you are applying.

You can display your education in a similar way. Under "Education," include degrees completed or in progress. If appropriate, add another category, "Additional Coursework and Training," in which you list courses that highlight knowledge and skills you've acquired through training seminars or the like that are relevant to the position.

If you have a friend who is a designer, you might ask for help with choosing a typeface and layout. However, avoid an overdesigned resumé that appears contrived and cluttered. Also, if you are e-mailing your resumé, be sure to choose a font that the employer will be sure to have installed on their computer. Most importantly, avoid including any personal information, such as age, weight, marital status, number of children, or even hobbies on the resumé or in the cover letter.

If it is appropriate for employers to view examples of your work, consider including a link to those samples on your resumé. For instance, if you're exploring job opportunities as a graphic artist or a writer for Web sites, you may want to build your own Web site that displays your work. Include your Web address on your resumé with a notation such as "to view my portfolio" or "for examples of my work, please visit." If you are posting your resumé online, establish a link to your Web site.

Use your informed contacts and job listings to determine the best way to send your resumé. Some employers require resumés sent by mail. Others welcome resumés sent electronically, either as e-mail attachments or as part of the text of the e-mail. Read up on correct formatting techniques so your resumé translates clearly. Although resumés can also be faxed, legibility can be a problem. But if a job posting has a fast-approaching deadline, you might consider e-mailing or faxing your resumé, then following up by sending a copy in the mail.

If you have not heard from the employer after a week or two, it is appropriate to send an e-mail or fax or leave a voicemail message, providing the job description listed a phone number and the company encourages phone calls. Ask if your resumé and cover letter have been received. Resumés and cover letters sometimes do get lost, accidentally deleted, or misfiled. Following up can bring this to the employer's attention, and it demonstrates your continued interest in the position.

Use *The Riley Guide* and the other resources in this journal (page 158) to find tips on writing a resumé. Read discussions on the best format to use, such as chronological, functional, or a combination, and review several examples to pick up ideas. Ask people in your support network or some of your informed contacts if they'd read your resumé and give you feedback.

To compose a draft of your resumé, draw from the work and education history that you listed previously.

{the unplanned career}

Writing a Cover Letter

"I consider it a good rule for letter writing to leave unmentioned what the recipient already knows, and instead tell him something new."
—SIGMUND FREUD

The cover letter represents you in your absence and personalizes your job search. Since it is not always possible to hand-deliver your resumé, the cover letter states what you would say in person to an employer. Limited to one page, it should include four main points: the name of the position for which you're applying, your strongest qualifications for the position, your knowledge of the company or position, and a request to be contacted.

Researching the position will allow you to tailor your cover letter to the position. Review the job description for key words and include them in your discussion of your qualifications. Some larger companies electronically scan cover letters and resumés for such words to establish your qualifications.

Keep your cover letter concise and precise. The first paragraph should identify the name of the position, which is especially important when more than one position is available. If someone referred you to the position, mention the person's name in this paragraph, or cite the periodical or job posting service where you found the listing. Make your point directly, for example, "I am applying for the position of hotel manager advertised in the *Post*." Or, if you have been referred by someone, "Sarah Smith, Art Director at J. Langston Design, suggested that I apply for the advertised position of display artist." Resumés frequently are separated from cover letters during the review process. Including the name of the position on both can help in the screening process.

While you can reference your resumé in your cover letter, avoid repeating information found there or including lists of your qualifications. Instead, mention your strongest qualifications in the second and third paragraphs. For example, don't write, "As you can tell from my resumé, I have worked as a manager at Lawton Electric, Marvis Plumbing, and Watkins Construction." Instead, state, "During the past several years, I have managed the acquisitions department in the electrical, plumbing, and construction industries."

Also within these middle paragraphs, emphasize your professional growth, for example, "Over the last two years, I have been promoted from assistant buyer responsible for one store to senior buyer in charge of fifty regional stores." Include one or two accomplishments that demonstrate your qualifications. If you improved or changed something, point this out: "I successfully avoided a costly strike by negotiating a salary and benefits package that was acceptable to line staff and management."

These two central paragraphs can contain a fact or two that you discovered through your research of the company. If a company is developing a location overseas, you might mention how your bilingual skills or global business experience or studies can benefit the company's international business plan.

The concluding paragraph simply and directly expresses your request for contact: "I look forward to meeting with you to discuss my qualifications. I can be reached by e-mail or by phone at [include address and number]." Although your contact information is listed on your resume, state it in the body of the cover letter for the reader's convenience and in case the cover letter is separated from the resume.

Employers look closely at how your cover letter is written as well as at the points you make within it. A well-written letter reflects not only your qualifications but also your attention to detail, such as spelling, grammar, and sentence construction, which are among the skills employers value in candidates. Always have someone proofread your cover letter before you send it out. Whether you are sending it by traditional mail or electronically, ask someone in your support network to review it and offer comments.

The format you use will vary according to how you send your cover letter. You'll need to follow a traditional business format if you are sending your letter through the mail. If you are sending it via e-mail, either as an attachment or in the body of the e-mail, you will need to format it differently. Consult the resources at the back of this journal for examples of cover letters formatted in plain text (often the case for those sent electronically) and for letters written to be scanned. Note especially what the resources state about attachments. Some employers prefer cover letters and resumés in the text of an e-mail rather than as attachments. Attachments can be difficult to open and raise concerns about computer viruses.

Give yourself plenty of time to compose your cover letter. First make an outline on the following page, listing the points you will include in each paragraph. Then, create a draft on pages 93–95, using your outline as a guide. Be sure to ask someone in your support network to review the initial draft before you compose the final.

Cover Letter Outline:

Introductory Paragraph

Middle Paragraph 1

Middle Paragraph 2

Concluding Paragraph

Draft of Cover Letter:

Selecting References

"A little praise / Goes a great ways. . . ."
—RALPH WALDO EMERSON

Employers usually want to know in advance of hiring you what kind of a worker you'll be. They expect to gather that information by contacting people from a list of references you provide. Therefore, it's important to think carefully about the people you'll select for your list. Your reference list should contain the names of people who can speak to your work abilities and relevant qualities. Even if you have little or no work history, you can still select references.

A reference can be a former boss, coworker, teacher, or counselor. Avoid family members because employers will not consider them objective. You can compile a list of names to give to potential employers if you are asked, or you can have copies of reference letters prepared to submit. Be sure to find out if employers have a preference.

If you prefer not to list a former boss, select a coworker or a supervisor from another department who is familiar with your work. If you lack paid work experience, use the names of people for whom you volunteered or interned, or teachers and counselors who can speak to your reliability, motivation, accuracy, kindness, and other qualities an employer will value.

If you are currently employed, consider your customers or the people at other companies you work with as potential references. At the end of key projects—or, if appropriate, when you are leaving a job—ask these people if they would be willing to serve as references or write reference letters for your files.

References are given not only in written form, such as form letters or formal reference letters. A potential employer may call or e-mail your references to ask about your work performance. Although the legal guidelines in some states limit what a former employer can say to verifying your job titles or the dates you worked, a reference that is reluctant to answer other questions may reflect poorly on you. Therefore, consider preparing your reference for a potential employer's contact.

Call everyone you intend to use as a reference and describe the position for which you're applying. Write out the qualities or skills you'd like each reference to mention if you think something might be overlooked. People are generally not offended by such directness; they may welcome it, because it will be easier to know what to say about you, and they want to represent your best qualities. For a phone script, make a list of bulleted points. When people are rushed or caught off guard, they may inadvertently omit important information or include information that does not help you. To assist a reference responding to an e-mail, it might be best to draft a full e-mail instead of providing bulleted points.

Record the names and contact information of people you'll ask to be references along with any reminders about what you want them to say to potential employers.

{the unplanned career}

{the unplanned career}

Interviewing Thoughtfully

Remember one thing about getting ready for an interview: You are not preparing for an interrogation; you are preparing to talk as one equal to another about a mutually interesting topic—you and your areas of curiosity. If you worry about how you'll do on an interview, here are some steps you can take to feel prepared and confident.

The first step, and in many ways the most important, is developing a new attitude about the interview as a thoughtful conversation. It is an opportunity to discuss the work you've done and the skills you possess. Confidence comes from feeling secure about your skills and what you have accomplished, whether in a paid job or as a volunteer or intern.

In an interview, the spotlight is on you to advocate for yourself through well-prepared answers to interview questions. Anticipate questions that might be asked, such as, "Tell us about one accomplishment you're the most proud of." Would it be the staffing problem you solved or a good budgetary decision you made? Was it the deadline you met despite all sorts of obstacles or the satisfying of a disgruntled customer whom no one else could please? Let your examples reveal who you are and what you care about.

Suppose you're asked, "Why should we hire you?" Answering this question is an opportunity to demonstrate that you know about the company or agency through a prior informational interview or other research you've done before the interview. Use a few select examples to show how your qualifications will suit the position that the company or organization is seeking to fill.

You might be asked about your work style. For example, an employer might want to know if you are self-motivated and can work with little supervision. Or you might be asked about your willingness to work with a team of people. To address these points, an interviewer might say, "Describe a project you worked on and your role in the project," or "Describe a problem you solved and how you involved others in the solution." Your answers can indicate your personal initiative and ability to work with others.

Practice your answers aloud before the interview so you'll be comfortable talking about yourself. If you sound rushed or nervous, perhaps you need to include fewer points in your answer. Ask people in your support network to pose questions and give you feedback on your answers.

It's natural to be nervous in an interview, but there are some things you can do to manage your nervousness. Before you answer a question, pause to be sure you understand what the question is asking. If you need a little time before you answer, ask the interviewer to repeat the question. Don't feel you have to rush your answer. Try to have a beginning and an end to your answer in mind before you start. Be patient with yourself and speak at your normal pace.

The topic of money may come up in an interview and will definitely need to be addressed before you accept a position. Before the interview, consult the job description and other resources and determine a salary range for your position. Factor in your experience and come up with a range that you would quote to an employer if asked what salary you'd accept. For additional help with this topic, consult the Resources section of this journal (page 158).

At the end of each interview, many employers ask if you have any questions. Ask no more than two questions, because most employers have other applicants waiting, and be sure the questions clarify a point for you or help you assess if the job is right for you.

Note the questions you anticipate being asked on interviews and jot down the answers you'd give. Rehearse the answers aloud before interviews and rewrite your answers as necessary.

Keep Going

"Step by step."
—CHINESE PROVERB

When you're searching for a job, even one that is a natural outgrowth of your curiosity, you will likely become discouraged, especially if you are putting in a lot of effort with very little return in the beginning. Stay mentally and physically healthy by eating right, exercising, and surrounding yourself with encouraging people. Check in periodically with the people in your support network and talk with them about your progress. Be sure to go back through your journal and read your own words for encouragement. Do additional informational interviews if you feel stuck looking for a position. Talking to new people can refresh your ideas and revitalize your exploration.

Write down your ways to encourage yourself, nurture your enthusiasm and optimism, and stay healthy. Note the people you'll contact for support.

"Each step upward makes me feel stronger and fit for the next step."

—Mohandas K. Gandhi

{Chapter 4}
Growing in Your Work

As you work in your area of curiosity, you'll continue to grow. In many ways taking a job is just the beginning. Eventually your responsibilities will shift, your interests will evolve, and your personal life will change—and the position won't fit you as well as it did when you began. You may grow tired of your job and want to do something else. Or you may wish to take on new responsibilities that interest you, but you may not be sure how to manage the new workload or ask for a promotion.

The changes you'll go through in your work are normal, because you are constantly developing. If you act on the changes, you can create exciting opportunities. That's where this chapter will be of help. Use this journal to guide you as you grow in your work or prepare to leave your job for something new. Remember that this process is a circle where endings merge with beginnings.

Reviewing Your Own Progress

"Life teaches us to be less harsh with ourselves and with others."
—GOETHE

Make an effort to take action when you notice that you're changing or that the work you're doing is changing. If you don't, you run the risk of losing your enthusiasm and, most importantly, your curiosity. To aid you in recognizing the changes you're going through, it helps to do a review of your own performance in your work. Reflect on the following questions, which will help you review your progress before you decide on a course of action.

How have you changed since you began in your current work? Do some tasks drain you of energy while others invigorate you? Can you explain why?

What external factors—such as a new boss, a new schedule, or added responsibilities—have transformed your position? How has the change, or even the lack of change, affected your attitude?

{the unplanned career}

How would you describe your performance in your work? At what tasks do you excel? Are there areas you could improve? If you would prefer to do different things, what might they be?

Take a few moments every three months to do your own performance review by recording what you've done and what you've learned in the process. Whether you've been in your job six months or six years, keep track of how you think you're doing. Note what you like doing and what you don't. Consider areas of your job that are becoming stale and the more rewarding activities you'd prefer in their place. If you notice that you or your work has changed, consider taking action to turn those changes into opportunities to grow.

Date:

Date:

Date: _____

_____

_____

_____

_____

_____

_____

_____

_____

_____

Date: _____

Date:

Date:

{the unplanned career}

Date:

Date:

Date:

Preparing for a Performance Review

"Very often it happens that a discovery is made whilst working upon quite another problem."

—THOMAS ALVA EDISON

In a performance review, your boss evaluates your work after you've been in your position for a certain period of time. When you first begin work, an initial review might be scheduled after three or six months, followed by regular reviews every year or upon promotion. At other jobs, it may be up to you or your boss to schedule reviews as needed. By the time of review, both you and your boss will have become familiar with your work performance. Most importantly, you will have had an opportunity to see what you might like to learn so you can keep your curiosity alive in your work.

In a typical review, you listen to your boss describe your performance and you hope you'll be able to keep your job or get a promotion, or even a raise. As you'll discover in this journal, the performance review can be much more than just a one-way conversation in which your boss does all the talking. The performance review, like the employment interview, can be a thoughtful conversation, meaning that you'll have a much more active role in the process.

If your boss has not scheduled a review with you and you've been in your position for some time, ask to set a date. Performance reviews can easily get pushed to the bottom of your boss's to-do list. If you've been working for several months or even several years and want to check in about your progress, don't wait for your boss to suggest a review—take the initiative yourself.

Before your meeting, write down the topics you'd like to discuss. As an active participant in your review, you shouldn't feel that you have to defend yourself. You're preparing to review the past, discuss the present, and create an exciting future.

Use the following questions to help you prepare for the performance review.

Can you anticipate the positive and negative points about your work that your boss will likely emphasize? Prepare a response, keeping it thoughtful and reflective. If you've made some mistakes, discuss them as learning experiences and describe how you've benefited.

What strengths do you want to discuss? List them so you can mention them in case your boss doesn't. Talking about what you do well is not bragging; it's presenting the truth.

When you reviewed your own progress, did you discover activities that you'd like to do but are not part of your work—and that you want to discuss with your boss? Conversely, what would you like to do less of?

Analyzing Your Review

"I have come to feel that the only learning which significantly influences behavior is self-discovered, self-appropriated learning."
—CARL R. ROGERS

After the performance review with your boss, you may want to take some quiet time to reflect on how it went. The sooner you do this after your review, the more you'll remember. Use the following questions to assist you. Remember to continue to review your own performance on a regular basis to ensure you are prepared for the next review.

What were the main points your boss stressed? What were your main points? Did you agree or disagree on similar points?

Were you satisfied with the results of the review? If not, what areas were left unresolved? Will you request a follow-up meeting to discuss these issues or review your progress?

Based on your review, what are your hopes for the future? What will you continue to do? What can you change so your next review will go better?

{the unplanned career}

Requesting a Promotion

"The rung of a ladder was never meant to rest upon, but only to
hold a man's foot long enough to enable him to put the other
somewhat higher."
—THOMAS HENRY HUXLEY

Asking your boss for a promotion can be difficult and awkward. Both you and
your boss bring different perspectives to the conversation. From your perspective,
wanting a promotion may come after you've learned as much as you can and
you're ready to do something else. Or maybe you've taken on added responsibilities
and feel that you've outgrown your current job title and deserve to be rewarded
for your work. Some see a promotion as moving up, while others see it as moving
sideways, especially if the promotion comes with more flexibility. Regardless of
the direction, a promotion means that you'll be adding new activities and responsibilities to your current job or assuming an entirely new position, perhaps one
where you manage people responsible for what you once did.

From your boss's perspective, promoting you means that you have excelled at
what you've done and you're ready to take on new challenges. If your performance
review is going well, that might be the perfect time to discuss a promotion. If
your boss brings up issues that need to be dealt with first, consider scheduling
a separate meeting after the review so you can demonstrate your progress. Even
if you haven't been at your job long enough to be promoted, use the review
process, if appropriate, to find out from your boss how you could be promoted.

Don't wait until your good work is noticed by your boss to ask for a promotion;
you could be waiting a long time. Take the initiative to bring up the subject.
During your performance review or another meeting with your boss, speak as if
you were already in the promoted position. For example, if you're seeking a
supervisory position, behave as a supervisor would. Use examples of systems
you'd put in place, for instance, and describe how you'll help prepare coworkers
for any changes. If you're interested in becoming a project manager, demonstrate
your knowledge or resources and your ability to juggle many responsibilities. Give
your boss a preview of how you'd think and act if promoted.

A temporary promotion can sometimes be beneficial for both you and your boss.
If your boss has reservations about promoting you, suggest a trial period. After a

few months in the new position, you'll know if you like the position or not. If you do, request a meeting with your boss to discuss your performance and request a permanent promotion.

Before you meet with your boss, write down the reasons you'll give for deserving a promotion. To come up with the best strategy, sketch out a script so you'll be sure to mention your strengths and achievements, and what you can bring to the position.

Asking for a Raise

"Be not afraid of going slowly, be afraid only of standing still."
—CHINESE PROVERB

Discussing money inevitably brings up feelings of worth. Making more money requires that you believe your work performance deserves it. A first step toward achieving that is to acknowledge that you have valuable skills and make important contributions. Be proud of your experience, no matter the duration.

When you ask for a raise will depend on the setting. At your workplace, raises may be given only after a set period of time or after you've taken a test and been placed in a promoted position. In these cases, your opportunity to receive a raise is limited to your experience and service time.

In other settings, you may have more flexibility. For example, it may be appropriate to ask for a raise after a favorable performance review or after completing a successful project. Do some investigating with your human resources manager, your coworkers, or your boss to find out how and when raises are given in your work setting.

Remember that you don't have to be promoted to earn more money. You may feel that you're underpaid for what you do. Do your homework and find out what people who do similar work earn. Consult the resources listed in this journal (page 158) to assist you in researching the range of salaries earned in your field.

If it's appropriate for your work setting, request a meeting to discuss salary ranges with your boss. If the raise your boss offers falls short of the high end of your scale, try to agree on how you might improve your performance to deserve the higher salary, and negotiate a future date for another increase.

Before you discuss a raise, practice what you'll say to your boss with people in your support network. Your voice tone and eye contact should convey your belief in yourself. Practicing ahead of time can help you feel and appear more confident.

Compose a list of reasons you deserve to earn more money. Write down a comfortable salary range and the sum you'd accept. Record your options if you do not receive a raise—for instance, discussing a schedule for when a raise would be possible or deciding to look for work elsewhere.

Redesigning Your Work

"I invent nothing. I rediscover."
—AUGUSTE RODIN

To keep your curiosity engaged in your work, you can redesign what you do by increasing the activities you enjoy and jettisoning those you don't. Among the other benefits, you can create opportunities to strengthen your skills, test out new interests, or collaborate with different coworkers. You might even use the redesign of your work as preparation for seeking different work in a new environment.

One way to begin redesigning your work is to think of new skills you'd like to acquire. Consider Sean, who still liked his work as a museum technician but felt it was growing monotonous. His position had two main responsibilities: proofreading the museum's publications and guiding museumgoers through the exhibitions, giving the same history each time. The museum management was negotiating with a firm to provide audio tours. For Sean, becoming involved in this transition would be an opportunity to invigorate and expand his knowledge of history and explore script writing. When negotiations were finalized, Sean asked his boss if he could work with the museum committee drafting the text for the audio tours. His boss consented, and Sean was able to apply his historical knowledge in a new context, pick up new skills, and explore another area of curiosity.

What new skills do you want to learn in your work? Do you foresee changes in your work setting in which you could participate? Sketch out your ideas, noting the new skills and experiences you want to gain. Before you discuss these ideas with your boss, outline the conversation, being sure to note how allowing you to learn new skills will benefit the company or organization.

{the unplanned career}

Another way to redesign your work is to think of a problem that needs solving. For example, Dolores had been observing that disability claims for repetitive stress had been rising. She approached her supervisor with a proposal to bring in health professionals to train people on workplace safety and ergonomics. Not only did this energize her curiosity about her work, but her new role coordinating safety seminars introduced Dolores to the field of occupational health. She is now studying the field and preparing for a new career.

What problems need solving in your work? Perhaps customer service is lacking at your workplace and you have an idea for training personnel. Or you might have thoughts on how to improve finances, implement better technology, market a product, or streamline meetings. Sketch out your ideas, highlighting your role. Outline the conversation you plan to have with your boss when you request these new responsibilities.

{the unplanned career}

Many bosses, no matter how much confidence they have in you, worry about who will do your work if you take on a new project or add new activities to your job. One trap to avoid is working two positions at once, which might cause you to become exhausted and discouraged. Before you initiate a conversation with your boss about redesigning your work, give some thought to how your current work could be modified. Consider various options for how work could be redistributed and how you can justify the changes you are proposing. Will the company benefit financially from your proposal, for example, and therefore be able to afford to hire extra help? Demonstrating that you have thought about the consequences of redesigning your work will be seen as an ability to solve problems.

Write down the ideas for modifying your work you will discuss with your boss.

Once you gain your boss's support and you begin working on a new project, implementing your ideas, or acquiring new skills through your new responsibilities and activities, send progress reports to your boss. Be specific not only about what you have gained but also about what you have contributed. If your new responsibility is a project with a specific beginning and end, create a summary of the results.

Sketch out the points you want to include in your progress reports.

The most important benefits of redesigning your work to expose yourself to new experiences and learn new skills are the insights you gain about how you'd like to continue developing your curiosity. For example, you now might want more opportunity to make decisions, or use your writing skills in your job, or work with technology. If it's appropriate in your work setting, you might want to meet with your boss to discuss further possibilities to arrange your current job so you can gain more new skills and experiences.

Reflect on how you'd like to continue to develop yourself and your curiosity in your work and record your thoughts. Compose a conversation you'd like to have with your boss to discuss the next stages of redesigning your work.

Looking Outside Your Work

"The purpose of life on earth is that the soul
should grow—so grow! By doing what is right."

—ZELDA FITZGERALD

By now, you may have exhausted your ideas and opportunities for developing yourself in your work. Each day you might think that it's time to go somewhere else, but you may not be ready to leave your work. Nevertheless, you can't ignore your need to grow and learn. One solution is to look into options outside your work to keep your curiosity alive and gain new skills and experiences. Through part-time opportunities, volunteering, continuing education, and/or freelance work, you can explore new areas of curiosity and prepare to leave your work by creating new contacts and possibilities.

It's tough to add more work to your already busy schedule, but taking on new activities while working a full-time job can invigorate you. Part-time work doesn't always mean half of a full-time job. It could entail only a few hours a week, especially if you do independent contracting or consulting.

Through your current or previous work, you might have met clients or customers whom you could tap as potential sources for part-time or freelance work. For example, Sam worked in a home improvement store selling plumbing and electrical supplies. While talking with a customer one day, he learned that his customer, a general contractor, was interested in hiring people to help out at his building site by procuring materials and cleaning up the site. Sam was curious about the field of construction, so he asked if he could work part-time. By adjusting his schedule at the store, Sam worked on the construction site Saturdays and one day a week before work. Not only did his income increase but he learned more about the field and made new contacts. He went on to apprentice with a contact made through that experience.

Businesses that you frequent can be another source of part-time work. Laurel had grown tired of her position as a hospital administrator but was not ready to quit her job. She had a growing curiosity about owning a business one day and needed a way to learn about running a business while employed full-time. A small boutique opened in her neighborhood, and Laurel approached the owner for a part-time job on Saturdays. These few hours a week gave her insight into operating her own small business.

If you have developed a skill through your work and you want to apply it in a different setting, consider doing freelance work or independent consulting. Your place of employment might be a source to investigate part-time opportunities. If your employer is about to contract out for a service and it's one you could provide, arrange with your employer to perform the work. Some employers don't care when you work on such outsourced jobs, as long as you meet the deadline. This opportunity could increase your income and give you additional experience and skills. Many companies allow employees to investigate other interests by interning in another department for a few hours or a day or two a week. This can be a way for a company to retain good employees.

To avoid laying off their employees during hard economic times and to improve their community relations, some companies offer to pay employees 50 percent of their salary if they volunteer for certain organizations such as schools and other nonprofits. This is an excellent opportunity to apply your skills and learn about different careers while still receiving a partial salary. Regardless of economic conditions, you can approach your company about such an opportunity.

Many companies offer a tuition reimbursement plan for employees completing their degrees. Although the guidelines usually specify which courses and degrees will be funded, general education classes and some electives are usually included. You can select courses that both meet requirements and allow you to explore your curiosity. Some companies fund certification programs offered by vendors or colleges. Such programs in technology, management, and other areas, lasting a year or less, are a great way to learn new skills and make new contacts.

You'll find many opportunities outside your regular work. If you have an interest in graphic design, could you do small jobs in the evening that would give you experience to list on your resumé and examples for your portfolio? If a friend at a company is launching a new product or service, could you be hired to work on it for a few hours on weekends? Note your ideas for outside opportunities and the people you will contact to pursue them.

{the unplanned career}

Moving On

—MARY, QUEEN OF SCOTS

You may reach the point when you've done everything you can to make the most of your position and no opportunities at work or additional part-time activities can hide that it's time to move on. Leaving a job is never easy, yet you can't stay if the work no longer fits you. The costs to your mental and physical well-being, as well as to your career and your curiosity, are too great.

You might go through various stages before you're ready to leave. For example, when you think that the position you've outgrown suddenly becomes "not so bad after all," you have fallen into a trap. Perhaps you'll try to convince yourself that what you have is better than anything else you'll find. This is the time to review what you wrote in your journal in Chapter 1, "The Unplanned Career," about myths, restraining thoughts, and the importance of your curiosity. You'll find encouragement in your own words.

Don't lose sight of the causes for your dissatisfaction. Give yourself credit for everything you did to improve your work, and accept that leaving is a beginning. As you prepare to leave your job, write down your reasons. Follow these thoughts with reflections on the beginnings you'll create. Note the people in your support network you'll contact to gain encouragement and those informed contacts who can help you take the next step.

{the unplanned career}

Exiting Gracefully

"Good to begin well, better to end well."

—JOHN RAY

Just as there are steps to take to begin your work, there is a process to follow when you leave. Make an effort to avoid quitting because you're angry. Instead, wait until your anger passes so you can think through how you want to leave. Depart with the graciousness that you admire in others who have made the same transition.

Anticipate the bases you'll need to cover, for instance, how much notice to give and the people to inform. If appropriate, offer to train or coach your replacement, or to turn projects over to people who are prepared to continue them. Let clients or customers know about the change, introduce your replacement, and reassure people that they'll be taken care of. This will preserve your reputation and pave the way for you to request references from former satisfied customers or clients.

If you have a good relationship with your boss, ask for a letter of reference before you leave. You may also want to ask a coworker or a supervisor in another department to write a letter.

End your working relationships positively. Tell people whom you respect how you benefited from working with them and mention what you learned. Thank them for their friendship and their kindness, and make arrangements to keep in touch— perhaps adding them to your support network or list of informed contacts.

As you prepare to leave your position, reflect on the experiences you had and the skills you gained. Write about these in your journal. Note the most important skills you developed and the contacts you made. Also record any new curiosities you developed but were unable to explore in your work that may lead to new opportunities.

{the unplanned career}

Jump into the Circle Anytime

"We shall not cease from exploration / And the end of all our exploring / Will be to arrive where we started / And know the place for the first time."

—T. S. ELIOT

The verse from T. S. Eliot is a reminder that exploring is essential at every stage of life. Exploration will keep you learning and growing in your work.

Remember that you can jump back into the circle of this journal anytime. You won't be starting over or wasting time—on the contrary, your own words will guide you and inspire you to move forward.

As you progress through your career, you may need to modify a choice you made or adjust what you're doing so it's a better fit. You can learn from your own words how to redesign your work by reviewing Chapter 4, "Growing in Your Work." If you begin to outgrow your work, review Chapter 1, "The Unplanned Career," for ideas on engaging your curiosity again. Or if you are ready to leave your job, turn to Chapter 4 for guidance and to Chapter 2, "Taking Action," and Chapter 3, "Directing Your Job Search," for steps to find another position.

Katherine Butler Hathaway said, "There is nothing better than the encouragement of a good friend." In many ways this journal is like a friend you can count on. Your own words will encourage you to keep developing your interests by following your curiosity. When you take action on your curiosity, you'll create opportunity.

Resources

The resources here are intended to support your exploration. Consider them a "sampler." You'll note from the titles below that you can find career ideas and inspiration from a number of different areas.

Selected Books

Bayles, David, and Ted Orland. *Art and Fear: Observations on the Perils (and Rewards) of Artmaking.* Santa Cruz, Calif.: Image Continuum Press, 1993. Unravels with humor the many myths that block people from doing creative work.

Bradbury, Ray. *Zen in the Art of Writing: Releasing the Creative Genius Within.* New York: Bantam Books, 1990. Not just for writers, but for everyone wanting to reclaim their curiosity. This is Bradbury's recounting of how he stood up to those who laughed at his interests and as a result forever unleashed his creativity.

Bridges, William. *Jobshift: How to Prosper in a Workplace without Jobs.* Menlo Park, Calif.: Addison-Wesley, 1994. Shakes up the customary view of having a job and replaces it with exciting and liberating alternatives.

Bronson, Po. *What Should I Do with My Life?* New York: Random House, 2002. This masterful book unfolds the stories of fifty people and reveals life themes that emerged about the struggles and triumphs involved in creating a satisfying life.

Carlson, Richard. *Don't Sweat the Small Stuff at Work.* New York: Hyperion, 1998. This follow-up to the best-selling *Don't Sweat the Small Stuff . . . and It's All Small Stuff* provides valuable tips for building positive work relationships and developing a healthy work life.

Carson, Rachel. *The Sense of Wonder.* New York: HarperCollins, 1956. The author of *Silent Spring* eloquently describes how she taught her grandson to find wonder and curiosity in everyday things. Her words are surrounded by the beautiful photography of Nick Kelsh. People who need a curiosity boost will find it here.

Gill, Brendon. *Late Bloomers.* New York: Artisan, 1996. Short descriptions of the lives of people (many you'll recognize) whose careers blossomed, and in some cases began, when they were in their forties or fifties, or older.

Graber, Steven. *The Everything Cover Letter Book.* Holbrook, Mass.: Adams Media Corporation, 2000. In addition to offering an excellent discussion of cover letter basics and sample letters for numerous career fields, this book includes useful tips for writing resumés and interviewing. Provides a good listing of job-hunting Web sites for specific fields.

Kelley, Tom, and Jonathan Littman. *The Art of Innovation.* New York: Doubleday, 2001. The inventors of such devices and products as the Palm handheld computer share how to keep inspiration and innovation alive. Good chapter on "expect the unexpected."

Kennedy, Joyce Lain. *Cover Letters for Dummies.* New York: Hungry Minds, 2000. Helpful critiques of various cover letters with a good discussion on points to include in each paragraph. Useful section on skills identification.

——. *Resumés for Dummies.* New York: Hungry Minds, 2000. Provides critiques of resumés for various career fields and experiences. Helpful formatting pointers for preparing traditional resumés and those for e-mail and scanning.

Lindsay, David. *House of Invention: The Secret Life of Everyday Products.* New York: Lyons Press, 2000. The history of some common inventions, many created by people who acted on unexpected opportunities.

Lloyd, Carol. *Creating a Life Worth Living.* New York: HarperPerennial, 1997. Inspirational interviews with people who have pushed through blocks to reach creative and meaningful work.

McCall, Karen, *MoneyMinders.* San Anselmo, Calif.: Financial Recovery Press, 2002. This workbook includes exercises and techniques to overcome money patterns that no longer work for you.

McKay, Matthew, and Patrick Fanning. *Prisoners of Belief: Exposing and Changing Beliefs That Control Your Life.* Oakland, Calif.: New Harbinger Publications, 1991. Ways that people can release themselves from limiting thoughts and myths.

Stanny, Barbara. *Prince Charming Isn't Coming: How Women Can Get Smart about Money.* New York: Viking, 1997. The author weaves together advice, anecdotes, and her own story to create an informative experience for readers.

——. *Secrets of Six-Figure Women: Surprising Strategies to Up Your Earnings and Change Your Life.* New York: HarperCollins, 2002. Based on extensive interviews of more than 150 women who earn over six figures, this book provides guidance for earning more money.

Selected Web Sites

There are inherent problems with listing Internet sites because they often change or disappear. To address this concern, I include *The Riley Guide*, a comprehensive site that has been around for some time and is constantly updated by research librarian and Internet expert Margaret Dikel (formerly Margaret Riley). If you have trouble locating sites that I've listed, *The Riley Guide* is a good place to find links to additional sites.

Backdoor Jobs: www.backdoorjobs.com
Information on how to obtain short-term employment. Of interest to those who want to explore an area of curiosity or ways to gain new skills without a long-term commitment.

www.craigslist.org
Primarily for those living in large cities, this site offers job listings by occupational field and posts resumés of those applying for various listings.

MonsterTrak's Virtual Interview: interview.monster.com/virtualinterview/campus
Simulates an employment interview by asking questions with multiple-choice answers. Comments on the strengths and weakness of each choice.

Occupational Outlook Handbook: www.bls.gov/oco
Introduction to occupational fields, with short descriptions of the work, training/education needed, pay, and much more.

The Riley Guide: www.rileyguide.com
Career information, resumé and interview tips, salary information, and much more. A megasite that links to numerous career and job search resources.

Salary Wizard: www.salary.com
Pay ranges for various career fields and jobs.

Volunteering: www.nonprofits.org or www.idealist.org
Two sites with volunteer opportunities.

Acknowledgments

A book goes through many stages before it is created. I want to thank and acknowledge those who contributed to the creation of this book.

I want to thank Nicole Stephenson for having the vision for this journal. I am grateful to Leigh Anna Mendenhall, Judith Dunham, Christina Amini, and others at Chronicle Books for shaping the journal through their thoughtful editing.

To my many clients and students who taught me how careers are really created, thank you for your wisdom and optimism.

I thank all of my friends for their encouragement, especially Karen McCall, for sharing her expertise about money and careers.

Lastly, I want to thank the most important person in my life, my life partner, Kathryn Hile, for her love, support, and encouragement throughout this process. Thank you for keeping my spirits high through your never-wavering belief in my ability to write this book.

Notes

{notes}

{notes}

{notes}

{notes}